E
743
.F73
1982

THE PRESIDENTIAL PRESS CONFERENCE

Its History and Role in the American Political System

Blaire Atherton French
The White Burkett Miller Center of Public Affairs

UNIVERSITY
PRESS OF
AMERICA

LANHAM • NEW YORK • LONDON

Copyright © 1982 by

University Press of America,™ **Inc.**

4720 Boston Way
Lanham, MD 20706

3 Henrietta Street
London WC2E 8LU England

All rights reserved

Printed in the United States of America

Library of Congress Cataloging in Publication Data

French, Blaire Atherton.
    The presidential press conference.

    Includes bibliographical references.
    1. Presidents–United States–Press conferences. 2. Press and politics–United States. 3. United States – Politics and government–20th century. I. Title.
E743.F73   1982   353.03'5   81–40883
ISBN 0–8191–2064–2 (pbk.)   AACR2

All University Press of America books are produced on acid-free paper which exceeds the minimum standards set by the National Historical Publications and Records Commission.

PREFACE

With the generous support of the John and Mary R. Markle Foundation, the White Burkett Miller Center of Public Affairs established a National Commission on Presidential Press Conferences. Under the co-chairmanship of former Virginia Governor Linwood Holton and RCA Vice President Ray Scherer, and using a wealth of material--including 600 pages of transcript from a series of preliminary meetings with White House correspondents, bureau chiefs, editors, and presidential press secretaries--collected by the Miller Center staff, the Commission issued recommendations aimed at improving the presidential press conference.

The Commission took pride in the fact that press secretary James Brady announced at President Reagan's first press conference that the administration intended to organize its conduct of presidential press conferences on the basis of the Commission's proposals.

Because of the strong interest generated by this report, the Miller Center determined to undertake a more detailed and analytical study of the press conference. The project was undertaken by a brilliant young political scientist, Blair Atherton French. It is hoped that this study will contribute to an increased understanding of this national institution, and thereby provide even greater support for the recommendations found in the Commission's report.

ACKNOWLEDGEMENTS

    I wish to thank Dr. James S. Young, who gave unstintingly of his time and expertise through this manuscript's many stages. I also wish to thank Dr. Kenneth W. Thompson for his enthusiastic interest in my work, and for providing research and administrative support from the White Burkett Miller Center of Public Affairs. Dr. Steven Rhoads contributed many helpful suggestions, for which I am grateful. I wish also to thank my husband, James Ceaser, for his steadfast encouragement and valuable contribution of ideas.

                                          Blair Atherton French

INTRODUCTION

Herbert Hoover said in his first official meeting with the press as President that in fifty years time we would probably have developed the presidential press conference to perfection.[1] That was in 1929. Now, just over fifty years later, the presidential press conference is still with us. Has Mr. Hoover's prediction come true? This study does not attempt to measure the perfection of the present state of the art, nor does it presume to make recommendations for its improvements; that challenge has been taken up by the White Burkett Miller Center of Public Affairs at the University of Virginia. The study presented here is an attempt to place the presidential press conference into an analytic framework.

This little book explores the history of the presidential press conference; how and why it came to be as we find it today. What accounts for its current norms; when did certain traditions begin or end? The official meeting of the President with the press is now an institution in our political system. What is the reason for its persistence through the years? What functions does it perform and are they unique? There are the concerns and questions this paper addresses.

EVOLUTION OF THE PRESS CONFERENCE IN THIS CENTURY

Theodore Roosevelt was the first President to utilize the privately owned press as a means of frequent communication with the public. Wishing to make his office a "bully pulpit," he pursued influence over news as one means to that end. Theodore Roosevelt was the first to initiate close and continuous ties with reporters, and may be accurately called the founder of presidential press conferences. He brought the press into the White House literally as well as figuratively. The tale goes that he looked out his window one rainy day and saw a group of reporters manning their usual post by the White House gates. Their purpose was to question those coming and going from the White House and in that way to gather news or leads. When T. R. saw them miserable, wet, and cold, he ordered that there be a room in the White House set aside just for them.[2] In doing so, T. R. granted them a status they had never previously enjoyed and would subsequently never lose.

The presidential press conference under T. R. was firmly in his control -- he made all the rules. He made "off the record" statements, meaning that what he said could not be quoted or alluded to in any way. This stricture held even if the reporters received the same information from another source.[3] T. R. used "off the record" remarks to educate the reporters. He hoped to foster what he considered to be more accurate (and sympathetic) reporting; he also wished to flatter the correspondents by taking them into his confidence. Moreover, T. R. would "leak" information by allowing a story to be printed which did not reveal the source.[4]

As the first President to engage the press, T. R. enjoyed all the opportunities available to one who works without the constraint of precedent. T. R. picked and chose those he would allow to attend these sessions; he used the conference as an occasion for reward and punishment, screening out the reporters who were the least likely to be sympathetic to his policies.[5] The meetings themselves were also one-sided. T. R. talked (usually while under the blade of his barber's razor) and the press listened. It was more of a lecture than an exchange of questions and answers.[6] Although T. R. had called the press in from the cold, he did not allow the reporters to forget that they were the President's guests.

However, privileges the press enjoyed under T. R. became expectations under Taft. The presidential press conference was only one administration old when Taft came into office. Though a one-time newspaper reporter himself (or perhaps because of this), Taft was extremely reluctant to meet with reporters. His first month in office went by without holding a session with correspondents. Although the press conference had received the aggressive consideration of only one President, its disuse met with bitter criticism, especially since Taft did very little else to generate news. He went to the other extreme, sometimes killing stories.[7] Reporters complained. Taft's response was that he was not another T. R. but that he would "try to accomplish just as much without any noise."[8]

Woodrow Wilson came into office and picked up what Taft had allowed to fall away. Wilson shared T. R.'s view of the press conference as a channel for leadership of public opinion. He developed the press conference even further by holding meetings with White House reporters on a regular basis for the first two and a half years of his administration.[9]

Unlike T. R., however, Wilson did not take the initiative with the press -- he allowed the reporters to ask the questions and made no attempt to direct the discussion.[10] He believed it beneath the dignity of his office to exploit the press conference the way T. R. had done. Thus, he adopted the British format of the Prime Minister's appearance before Parliament. Another important practice established by Wilson was that all accredited reporters should have equal access to the conferences; he dropped T. R.'s practice of picking and choosing participants.[11] In doing so, Wilson abandoned the use of admission to his conferences as carrots and sticks over reporters. The combined effects of these two innovations was to reduce the influence of the President over the news generated within his conferences.

Though Wilson had never been enamored of the press, he felt that being accessible through press conferences was the duty of a leader in a democratic society.[12] Yet, in the last years of his administration, Wilson wanted to exert more influence over public opinion (especially on the matter of the League of Nations) and the evidence suggests that he found his press conferences too inflexible for this purpose. He turned to other means of communication with the people: addressing Congress in person; establishing and using for propaganda purposes - the Committee on Public Information until its demise in 1918; and going on a speaking tour across country in support of the League of Nations Treaty.[13] It is ironic that Wilson should become the victim of the practices he himself started, for he is responsible for the two features of the presidential press conference that, to this day, render it least pliable in the President's hands.

The press conference thus appeared to be moribund when Warren Harding came to office. But Harding revived it. For Elmer Cornwell, a scholar who has done exhaustive work on the history of presidential relations with the press, Harding's decision was crucial. Once his administration included the press conference as one of its official duties, these sessions with reporters became part of the routine of the executive office. Harding's most significant contribution, for Cornwell, was that he institutionalized the presidential press conference.[14]

Harding, an ex-newspaperman himself, continued Wilson's practice of regular sessions open to all accredited reporters. His press conferences met twice a week, on Tuesdays at 1:00 and Fridays at 4:00. By altering the time, he allowed the evening and morning papers each to take turns in breaking the main stories.[15] Apparently, Harding felt at ease with correspondents and gave them quite a free hand, at least initially. One White House correspondent described these conferences as follows:

> At a given hour fifty to one hundred correspondents would be admitted to the office of the Executive, half-surrounding him. The President would rise from his desk and face his examiners. Without preliminaries of any sort, the questions would be fired at the head of the Government, a score of them and oftentimes more.[16]

Thus, Harding not only reinstituted Wilson's frequency of meetings in the first two and one-half years, but maintained the same format as well.

The Harding administration also gave the presidential press conference some new features. The "White House spokesman" emerged as a technique for allowing the President to be quoted without assuming full responsibility for his statements.[17]

Harding's biggest break with the Wilsonian approximation, in the press conference, of the British Prime Minister's appearance before Parliament came at the outset of his administration. Harding announced that all reporters' questions were to be submitted to him in writing and in advance. The correspondents turned in their questions shortly before the conference began. Harding then looked them over and chose which he would address. The reasons the administration gave for this new practice were the vast increase in the number of reporters, both domestic and foreign (and thus too many questions), as well as the "problem of the conflicting interpretations that had been placed on presidential refusals to answer questions in the past ..."[18] By requiring written questions in advance Harding had done two things. First, he regained some of the control lost under Wilson -- like T. R., he could now influence what the news would be. Second, he had figured out a way to avoid the hitherto telling silences when faced with questions he could not or would not answer.

President Calvin Coolidge embraced the press conference as a routine presidential activity. Over the span of eight years, he held five hundred and twenty conferences, averaging 7.8 per month. Like his predecessor, he was sensitive to the needs of reporters. He, too, timed his sessions with an eye to the deadlines of morning and evening papers. He also concerned himself with the physical comfort of correspondents when they travelled with the President. Coolidge appreciated the press's desire for a steady diet of newsworthy information.[19] Coolidge was aware of the advantages good press relations can yield.

However, Coolidge was not one to surrender the ground Harding had recaptured. With Coolidge the press conference remained firmly under the President's control. For the most part, Coolidge gave background information with occasional off-the-record remarks.[20] Like Harding, he requested written questions, but went a bit further in asserting his authority. While standing before the reporters he would sift through their questions and conspicuously pass over certain ones. He would not merely look at one and ignore it; he would actually read it aloud and then, without any comment, stick it under the bottom of the pile. Newspapers began to report the questions which had suffered such treatment and to draw inferences on what the President's silences might mean. Coolidge stopped their printed speculations by telling them to desist.[21] Despite the apparent inflexibility of Coolidge's format, however, there were in reality many follow-up questions which the President yielded from the floor.[22]

With President Herbert Hoover came great expectations for the presidential press conference. On the day following his inauguration, Hoover met with reporters and said that he heralded a new phase of press relations. He told the reporters to elect their own committee to meet with the President for discussions on how they could improve the press conferece. Hoover was particularly eager to clear up what he called the "twilight zone" between quotable and background information.[23] He abolished the "White House spokesman" and allowed reporters to quote him. Usually, he would distribute handouts of a statement after he read it to the correspondents. He retained the requirement of written questions in advance.[24]

For the first 120 days of Hoover's administration, he held more frequent and regular press conferences than any President before or since. However, all hopes for the golden age of these sessions collapsed with the stockmarket just seven months after taking office.[25] Hoover began to make some changes, none of them anticipated in his earliest intentions. He broke the then established rule of equal access and followed T. R.'s practice of screening out those reporters he suspected. His conferences remained scheduled for twice a week but cancellations became increasingly frequent. By September of 1932 the presidential press conference had altogether vanished. Like Coolidge, he very obviously ignored questions. He outdid Coolidge's audacity; however, by denying he'd ever received certain questions despite reporters' assertions to the contrary.[26]

In reading Hoover's press conferences one finds a complete lack of any give and take between the President and reporters. Hoover would come in, read a few statements, say he had either not received any questions or that he was not prepared to answer the ones he did have, and promptly dismiss the reporters. It was seldom that he would take spontaneous follow-up questions. Most of his press conference accounts barely fill a page. T. R. was able to conduct one-sided sessions of this sort without hurting his relations with the press, but Hoover could not. Hoover had neither the personality nor the absence of tradition which T. R. enjoyed. Blatant, inconsiderate manipulation of reporters obliterated any good feelings between the two parties. By the end of Hoover's administration the presidential press conference was once again in decline.

Franklin Roosevelt's era marks the beginning of what Cornwell calls "the modern press conference." However, F. D. R.'s format was not truly innovative. He dropped the written question requirement, but a spontaneous question and answer session was no different from the way T. R., Taft, and Wilson had conducted their press conferences. F D. R.'s insistence upon the privilege of speaking off the record and giving background information was what almost every other President had demonstrated as well. F. D. R. occasionally handed out statements for direct quotation, and this also was usual practice. And he maintained Wilson's open-access policy for all accredited reporters. Yet, despite this continuity with his predecessors, F. D. R. said in his very first press conference, "I am told that what I am about to do will become impossible, but I am going to try it."[27]

F. D. R. held his press conferences twice a week, every week: nine hundred and ninety-two sessions, through war years and personal illness. He usually met with reporters in the Oval Office; thirty or forty correspondents would normally attend.[28]

Yet F. D. R.'s remarkable regularity alone was not what made his sessions with the press unique. His personality, at once engaging and awe-inspiring, his concept of political leadership, and his incredible breadth of knowledge about the way the American government operates -- all these factors made his press conferences successful occasions for influencing the news, educating the public and reporters, and persuading public opinion.[29]

F. D. R. maintained a measure of control over the press, as had most of his predecessors, by instructing reporters on what information they could quote or refer to and what could not be repeated to anyone, including their editors. He also conducted, for the reporters' benefit, press conferences that were essentially seminars in economics or governmental operations. Indeed, F. D. R.'s new programs and policies required extensive background briefings so that reporters could intelligently explain the President's plans to the public. But by being the teacher as well as the one who decided what information may be made public, F. D. R. was often able to get across his point of view to the public through the press. An aid to this exercise of presidential leadership was the great popularity of the President among reporters. He flattered them by taking them into his confidence, and that trust was rarely, if ever, broken. He would also tell humorous stories (off-the-record) for the reporters' benefit, ask them about their families, and in general demonstrate great warmth towards them personally. He referred to the White House press corps as his family.[30]

This is not to say, however, that F. D. R. could not be cruel. He once ordered a New York Times reporter to sit on a dunce stool in the corner. After that incident, all F. D. R. had to say to a reporter was "Why don't you go over and sit on the dunce stool?" to stop a particular line of questioning.[31]

With F. D. R. one finds for the first time references to a few planted questions by the President in his press conferences.[32] Usually, however, if he had anything he wished to say, he would open with a formal statement; roughly half of his meetings with the press began this way. Reporters gathered around his desk and could ask as many questions as they wished and on any topic. Mr. James Rowe, assistant to President Roosevelt, recently described the proceedings:

> They [the reporters] all came in and they ... I think they did it according to rank. Russ Young always asked the first question. After you got rid of the hierarchy then anybody could ask any question. And you could come back to the President. You could go two, three, four times ...[33]

F. D. R.'s advance preparations for his conferences were minimal -- his easy sweep of knowledge and the sustained contact with reporters through frequent sessions meant that he was continually on top of everything going on. Yet if he did not know an answer to a question he would simply say so or refer the reporter to other experts within his administration.[34] The Press Secretary, Steve Early, might come in to remind the President of one thing or another while F. D. R. was getting dressed.[35] Later in his administration, F. D. R. gathered James Rowe, Steve Early, and a few others together before a press conference and asked for general ideas, or for suggestions on how to handle a particularly knotty issue. The sessions usually lasted twenty to thirty minutes.[36]

Although Harry Truman, in his first presidential press conference, said that all of F. D. R.'s guidelines would remain in force,[37] changes did occur. Instead of holding his meetings twice a week, Truman met with reporters once a week. Moreover, attendance enormously increased. The events of the 1930's and 40's propelled the White House into the role of a formidable world power -- the number of reporters who now clamored for room in the President's office had shot up to one hundred and fifty.[38] As a result, in the spring of 1950 Truman moved his press conferences to the Indian Treaty Room in the Executive Office Building. There everyone could sit down. Truman not only wanted everyone to be comfortable, he also felt the sessions should have more formality.[39]

When the conferences moved to their new quarters, Truman also requested that reporters identify themselves and their affiliation. His purpose was to make each correspondent responsible for the questions he or she asked. What he had found was that politically sticky questions were being hurled at him from the back of the room by people he could never identify.[40] This new requirement and the move to the Indian Treaty Room were the two changes Truman cited in his last press conference as making true improvements.[41]

Truman was much more willing than his predecessor to allow himself to be quoted directly. At times, especially in the beginning, Truman would say what he did not mean to say, and the immediate ramifications demonstrate how much the President's press conference captured the world's ear. An ill-thought out remark about use of atomic weapons prompted Prime Minister Attlee to board a plane to Washington.[42]

In time Truman grew more cautious. One finds in him the same tendency one saw in Hoover -- a tendency to cut back on press conferences during times of crisis -- but Truman returned to his normal schedule when the particular situation was resolved. Though he allowed reporters to quote him, often what he said was too highly seasoned for their use.[43] His administration also saw increased use of radio and the growth of television technology. Truman allowed only occasional use of radio tapes for the purpose of delayed broadcasting.[44] He did, however, permit newsreel cameras to record his last press conference.

The increased size, formality, and public visibility of the presidential press conference placed extraordinary information demands on Truman. Thus, he put staff to work on bringing together information and he would hold briefing sessions prior to each conference. Toward the end of his administration the preparation process included compilation of possible questions and answers in a notebook. This practice continues.[45] In this process one also sees the role of a press secretary beginning to evolve.

A number of reporters who have covered presidents from F. D. R. to the recent administrations often give Truman's press conferences the highest marks of all. Veteran reporter Clark Mollenhoff liked Truman's format best because the switch to the Indian Room meant everyone could have a chance to ask a question. Seats were taken on a first come, first served basis; any correspondent who got there early would sit close up and count on being recognized.[46] William White, a White House correspondent from F. D. R. to Ford, said:

> [Truman] was salty, feisty, and sometimes incautious. I believe, however, that he imparted more solid and legitimate information with less impermissable self-serving than any of the others I have known.[47]

Truman has become for many the touchstone for presidential press conference nostalgia.

Merriman Smith, writing in the early years of the Truman administration, and James Pollard, in an article written near the end of Truman's tenure, both say the same thing: after Truman the press conference no longer existed as simply the prerogative of the President.[48] Cornwell says that Harding was the pivotal point, but at his time the conferences had not yet survived intense national and international crisis. By the end of Truman's time they had come through highly risk times with all their Wilsonian marks of open government intact. Through a depression and a world war the presidents had kept talking (except for Truman's sporadic silences) and reporters had kept asking questions. After F. D. R. and Truman, custom had entrenched the practice to the point of making its termination politically unwise and virtually indefensible.

Dwight Eisenhower took up the thread of greater presidential initiative and advanced one step. Like Truman, Eisenhower held his sessions in the Indian Treaty Room (over two hundred reporters now gathered for the press conferences[49]) and he allowed his press conferences to be taped for radio under the same ground rules. However, Eisenhower cut back on the frequency of these sessions to once every other week, and by the end of his first year in office he allowed the entire meeting to be taped for radio -- Truman never released more than two or three sentences.[50]

Eisenhower went even further in his attempts to speak directly to the people, by allowing television cameras to record the press conference for delayed broadcast. One reporter, looking back on that step, said that it marked the beginning of the press conference's "heavy present trappings and panoply."[51] Out went the last two rows of chairs and in went wooden platforms for the cameras. Those newspaper correspondents who had been long used to the old way saw T.V. and radio news men as "interlopers on their turf,"[52] and complained about the written media's diminished advantage. Not surprisingly, radio and T.V. people loved the new arrangements. Ray Scherer, an N.B.C. news correspondent at the time, urged Press Secretary James Hagerty to do live broadcasting. Hagerty refused. Eisenhower was too fearful of making an irrevocable slip.[53]

During Eisenhower's administration, presidential press conferences now made their appearance on the nightly news. With everything being recorded there was little reason left to prohibit exact quotations in print. Within an hour after a press conference, everyone would receive a transcript of the session.[54] Hagerty did say, however, that all direct quotations or recordings were subject to his approval or editing. He seldom chose to exercise this right.[55]

Reactions to Eisenhower's format, once it was established, were mixed. Reporters themselves got some mileage out of the T.V. cameras and radio tapes. Sarah McClendon, a correspondent who worked for a string of Texas newspapers, would give a different affiliation each time she received recognition. In this way she advertised each one.[56]

The limelight, however, rested primarily on the President -- televising the press conferences brought him more often and directly into the public eye. The increased importance of these sessions inspired Eisenhower to carry on the preparation procedures Truman started. Eisenhower held early morning staff meetings, generally three times a week. Hagerty's staff prepared suggested answers to questions they anticipated in the upcoming presidential press conference.[57] Scherer, a television correspondent during Eisenhower's administration, would meet with Hagerty, Merriman Smith, and a few other reporters on the morning of the press conference. Together they would discuss what the first topic would be. In this way, everyone knew what to expect at the outset.[58]

Some post-Watergate reporters believe that Eisenhower often escaped the tricky, embarrassing, or too prolonged question with professions of ignorance. Reporters who dealt with Eisenhower learned to preface their questions with a brief rundown of the facts and attempt to reconstruct for the President the current problem. In this way they hoped to get a direct answer.[59] Their efforts were not always rewarded.[60] Eisenhower evoked and liked to respond to large, all-encompassing questions, such as what constituted his world view.[61] Some reporters look back and are appalled with what Ike "got away with" by behaving in this way. Clark Mollenhoff writes:

> No President and White House of my acquaintance ever gave out at once so much and so little. It is a sobering thought, in the afterlight, speaking seriously, that one of the most popular Presidents in our history never once felt the truly hot breath of a truly determined and substantive investigative job directed at crucial national issues.[62]

The spirit which prevailed in journalism during Eisenhower's time, however, was quite different from that of today.

By the end of Eisenhower's administration one sees the press conference embracing media technology development within the context of firm presidential control. F. D. R. fashioned the presidential press conference into a powerful tool and Truman kept the edge sharp. Eisenhower, with the introduction of delayed televised broadcasts on the evening news, now honed it to a new fineness. The reporters, vastly more numerous than ever before, retained the initiative in asking questions, and they also enjoyed the spillover of publicity onto the correspondents themselves. For the most part, however, the presidential press conference was evolving in a direction away from their control. When the people could hear and see Ike in those sessions for themselves, then reporters lost a great deal of their role as filters, interpreters, and tutors. As they diminished in importance, the President grew. In Eisenhower's last press conference a reporter asked if the President thought journalists had been fair to him. Eisenhower replied, "Well, when you come down to it, I don't see what a reporter could do much to a President, do you?"[63] Whether they were fair or not was irrelevant -- in the final result the reporters served the purposes of the President.

With John Kennedy the presidential press conference grew into the form familiar today. Kennedy, like the two Roosevelts, came into office with an appreciation for the potentials of leadership of public opinion through the news media. Kennedy was also familiar with the techniques of correspondents. He had once been a reporter himself.[64] Kennedy was very much at ease with the idea of presidential press conferences. In this respect he was very much of a latter-day Roosevelt. Moreover, unlike any of his predecessors, J. F. K. met in the press many people of his own age.

Kennedy took the step Eisenhower would not -- he broadcast his press conferences live on television. His Press Secretary, Pierre Salinger, details in his account of those years how the two of them came to this momentous decision. The first factor was Kennedy's confidence in the way he came across on television; in this he was thinking back to his performance in the campaign debates. Second, the danger of misspeaking was always present, but Kennedy and Salinger thought that even if he made a mistake in a non-televised conference he would still be on record and have to make a retraction.[65] Moreover, Kennedy was willing to incur the risk for the gain of live broadcasting, which was the ability to address the public directly. J. F. K. felt that print media to be mostly Republican in their sympathies (the publishers of seven out of ten dailies had been for Nixon); hence, he wanted to present his Democratic policies to the people in a way that would effectively immunize the public from critical editorials.[66] Nor did he trust reporters. In a conversation with James Rowe over the danger of misspeaking on live television, J. F. K. said:

> There may be something to [your concern] but I am convinced that the press will turn against me sooner or later while I am President, and I must have a way to get to the American people. So, therefore, I have to use television to get there so I can speak directly to them when the press is so hostile.[67]

Not surprisingly, live television coverage brought objections from news people outside the T.V. media. Their objections were as follows: the press conference would be turned into a "sideshow" with reporters vying for the spotlight; as a result there would be no in-depth questioning; and the President might avoid answering a question if a reporter caught him off guard, whereas he might otherwise answer it if he had the time to pause over it.[68]

Salinger was not persuaded by these sorts of arguments. First of all, he said, questioning had not been in-depth since

Hoover's day. Moreover, he decided to cut down on any temptation to reporters to indulge in coast-to-coast advertising by dropping the practice of identifying oneself before asking a question. This particular change, rather than mollifying the press, angered them further.[69] Salinger believed the real reason reporters did not want live television was that it gave T.V. all the advantages. At least Ike's delayed broadcasts allowed the afternoon papers to break the story first.[70]

One other criticism from the press on this move was that live T.V. would turn the press conference into the podium of the President -- become a "propaganda tool" and thus no longer a true source of news.[71] To make it the mouthpiece of the President was indeed the aim of Kennedy and Salinger, but they hoped to do so without rendering it unnewsworthy. The public's attention was riveted to their young, confident, and knowledgeable President and the effect was as immediate as it was pervasive. Once the televised press conferences began, the mail response was tremendous. Most people who wrote were sympathetic to Kennedy over against the reporters. In a press conference of March, 1961, a reporter said the people believed the press were abusing Kennedy in their questions, not showing enough respect. He asked Kennedy essentially to get reporters off the hook.[72]

Everyone watched the President. Even the Soviet Union broadcasted excerpts of Kennedy's press conferences.[73] To accommodate the swell of correspondents (four hundred were in regular attendance) Kennedy held his sessions in the auditorium of the new State building. Salinger liked this room because he could partition off the back, depending on how many reporters attended. In that way the President always appeared to address a "full house."[74]

In recognition of the importance of his press conferences Kennedy had extensive pre-conference briefings, patterned after Eisenhower's. Press Secretary Salinger would meet with various department heads and together they came up with questions the reporters would probably ask. He would also prepare responses and a great deal of background material for particularly volatile issues. Kennedy would look over the questions and material at the end of the day preceding the press conference. The next morning there was a breakfast session with the Press Secretary, representatives of the departments of State, Treasury, Defense, as well as USIA, NASA, CIA, and the Atomic Energy Commission; and the Vice-President. They would rehearse questions. If Kennedy required more information, Salinger would give it to him after J. F. K.'s noon nap. The press conferences usually met at four o'clock.[75]

Though Kennedy held fewer conferences and with less regularity than Eisenhower, this fact is obscured by Kennedy's more intense impact. Kennedy, by virtue of his live broadcasts became a "personality." Some reporters in retrospect believe live coverage on television encouraged aggressive and superficial reporting; increased importance led to larger attendance which made for more competition among reporters and less in-depth reporting. Only the most loud and pugnacious got their questions in. Television cameras also may have fostered "softball reportorial pitches" or, worse, attempts to argue with the President -- neither extreme yielded useful information.[76]

Any benefits reporters could personally accrue from Kennedy's format were slight, however, when compared to those the President enjoyed. Without question he received the lion's share of attention, turning the whole affair into what reporter Robert Donovan called a "matinee."[77] One reporter who covered Kennedy's press conferences described what it was like to be in the correspondent's position. Pater Lisagor said,

> In Kennedy's time .. [the press conference] was a little like making love in Constitution Hall. In those days we did our yo-yo act in the large State Department auditorium. When we were recognized, we threw our questions across a vast expanse and that was the last contact we had with it, because the President fielded them a bit like Willie Mays and then turned to the cameras to make his responses.[78]

Correspondents had never before been reduced to such a prop-like role. No matter how much respect or authority other presidents had commanded or enjoyed, they still had to rely on the reporters to perform the role of an intermediary. With Kennedy, the presidential press conference became drama, and he was the star. The public got "the scoop" simultaneously with the press. The latter could no longer lay claim to the unique advantage of having been personally present.

Live television broadcasting is indeed a benchmark in the history of presidential press conferences, but it did not constitute a break with the past. The two Presidents before Kennedy had allowed their voices to carry directly to the public. Kennedy continued in the direction established by those before him.

Moreover, other practices associated with the presidential press conference became part of tradition in Kennedy's time. The sessions always began with a question by the UPI or AP senior correspondents; the senior wire service reporter also ended the conferences with a "Thank you, Mr. President."[79] It was still customary for senior correspondents to meet with the Press Secretary on the day of the conference to inform him of what sorts of questions the President could expect. In turn, the Press Secretary would indicate if the President would be making any major announcements. Salinger did not find this ritual to be in any way helpful, probably because he and his staff already anticipated what questions would be asked.[80]

Kennedy's graceful handling of the presidential press conference was a hard act to follow, yet Vice-President Lyndon Johnson was expected to do just that after Kennedy's assassination. Whereas J. F. K. molded the setting to work for him, L. B. J. had to prevent the whole event from working against him. He did not wish to be directly compared to Kennedy. Instead of using the State Department auditorium, his first televised press conference met in the International Conference Room in the same building. J. F. K. had stood behind a rostrum; L. B. J. preferred to sit behind a desk.[81]

The consensus among those who covered Johnson appears to be that he was not comfortable before the cameras. Ray Scherer believes the presidential press conference actually retrogressed during the Johnson administration; L. B. J.'s discomfort before the cameras inhibited the man and forced him to seek restlessly for some "ideal format."[82] James Rowe remembers Johnson when the president was at his ease:

> He was the most articulate, charming, persuasive fellow I have ever met. And if you walked in with a tape recorder on, he would become absolutely wooden.[83]

William White remembers on how L. B. J. "disliked and flinched from television, ... tending to freeze" before a camera. He goes on to say that Johnson "simply was not a press conference type of politician."[84] After only one presidential term of live televised press conferences, and not even a complete one at that, performance before the cameras became the standard by which one judged a President.

Johnson once drew criticism for the erratic times and places at which he held his sessions with the press. He responded:

> I will continue seeing the press at different times, different places, and different ways at my own choosing.[85]

Indeed, in his first 13 months, he held thirty-one press conferences: fourteen in the Oval Office; four in the Cabinet room; four in the State Department; four on his ranch in Texas (where a haybale served as a podium); one in the theatre of the White House; two while walking with reporters about the White House; and one was held as a picnic on the South Lawn.[86] In March of 1965 Johnson gave his own rendition of his press conferences:

> . . . eighteen off the record, eighteen . . . with adequate advance notice, sixteen covered by radio and T.V., eight live on T.V., nine informal lengthy walks with the White House press corps . . .[87]

L. B. J. was certainly one who liked to be unpredictable.

Doris Kearns, a White House fellow during the Johnson years and an informal confidant of L. B. J., maintains that L. B. J. eventually had to abandon his freewheeling style. In time he went back to the format of Kennedy. As she put it, "[The] evolution of the formal, televised press conference had gone too far to be stopped."[88] Measured in terms of time it seems to have not gone very far at all when it came to Johnson, but when measured in terms of expectations it had come quite a ways indeed.

With each president one can see how his press conferences are as much a reflection of his personality as they are products of established procedure and historical accident. Johnson's disposition was to take the 1964 landslide election to be a mandate for any policies he might favor. As Kearns has analyzed it, the election had an energizing effect -- Johnson had always been one to get his way in politics one way or another. Now he wished to dominate his press conferences.[89] Other presidents prior to L. B. J. enjoyed respect and the confidence of the reporters and public as a matter of course. Johnson's handling of the Vietnam War and the growing national concern over it was to place great stress on that unquestioning faith.

Pierre Salinger resigned as L. B. J.'s Press Secretary in March of 1964. In Salinger's book, <u>With Kennedy</u>, he describes Johnson's growing anger with the press as he encountered in his conferences questions that reflected suspicion and hostility towards his Vietnam policies. Salinger noted Johnson becoming secretive, not in the mode of Eisenhower's understatements, but in a way which seemed furtive and underhanded.[90]

Johnson is the best argument against the belief that the number of press conferences a President holds is an indication of his willingness to take the press or public into his confidence. He never cut down on the frequency with which he met with the press. Totalling one hundred and twenty-seven in all, he held his conferences roughly three times a month in 1964. In 1967 he still held them at least twice a month.

L. B. J. may have met with the press, but he effectively cut off any news. He began to open his conferences with long statements which, as one reporter remembers, "used to go on into interminable length [and which] didn't make a damn bit of difference."[91] These prepared remarks would often take up one-third to one-half of the allotted time; and the transcripts reveal long, boring programmatic breakdowns with a profusion of budget figures. One participant described his experience: "I was at a session once with Johnson where if he had said we're going to war tomorrow, I wouldn't have remembered it when I got outside."[92]

According to Kearns, after the first elected year Johnson spent less time in preparation for these sessions.[93] All indications are that he wanted to get away from these meetings, which provided him with no strings, to other more manipulative, or at least less publicly visible, means of getting his views across. While devaluing the press conferences he tried to use personal interviews as a means of reward and punishment.[94]

The years 1967 and 1968 saw, at least within the context of the presidential press conference, the invention of what is now commonly called "the credibility gap." By February of 1967 the halo over the Oval Office was losing its glow. Reporter Douglas Kiker described Johnson then as "arrogant and not to be believed." He went on to say, "The President grandly mixes truth, half-truth and nontruth and dares you to attempt to isolate them."[95]

Johnson's evasive tactics within his press conferences had two effects. The most immediate and shortlived was to make the televised sessions lackluster, uninformative, and boring. The public probably became less attentive as Johnson chose not to exploit it for its dramatic impact.

The second effect was more durable. Johnson's contradictory statements and actions with respect to the Vietnam war cracked open the Pandora's box of suspicion. The press conference gradually became the scene for more antagonistic and adversarial reporting. The correspondents started to lose, not only their awe of the office, but basic respect as well. Toward the end of Johnson's administration the tension in his press conferences was unrelenting.[96] Not since Herbert Hoover had a president's meetings with reporters been marked by so much distrust. However, things had changed since 1930; the press through the years had acquired unprecedented power of exposure and political education; its self-confidence had increased a hundred-fold, and they were ripe to take up Johnson's challenge.[97]

A Republican President need not have inherited Johnson's "credibility gap." Nixon, however, continued in subterfuge. Toward the end of his administration the gap of believability became a chasm of distrust between himself and reporters in their meetings together.

Despite L. B. J.'s initial experimentation, he had not dramatically added to or detracted from the traditional procedures of the presidential press conference. Yet some changes had occurred by the time Nixon took office. The practice of the Press Secretary and senior reporters meeting on the day of the conference no longer existed.[98]

Television had wrought some side effects. The President's conferences now ended abruptly (usually) after thirty minutes; stations would present these sessions as a "public service" program. The broadcast cost the networks, and if the conference spilled over thirty minutes, the further disrupted schedule cost them even more.[99] Therefore, the senior wire service correspondent no longer ended the questions when he deemed it appropriate to do so. Instead he took his cue from Ron Ziegler.[100]

Nixon chose to hold his press conferences in the East Room, which was known for its elaborate decor. Nixon liked the majestic effect; he addressed reporters against a backdrop of a blue curtain.[101] Rather than using a podium he often spoke before a stand-up microphone.[102] Nixon's frequency of press conferences would lead one to believe that scarcity is a sign of disdain for the practice. He insisted that press conferences were not the place to discuss most serious matters. In his first official meeting with reporters he refused to say what he planned to do about inflation. He said that neither domestic nor foreign affairs should be treated in "off-the-cuff responses in press conferences. . ."[103] One wonders what he did intend to talk about in these meetings.

Nixon held thirty-nine press conferences in all, fewer than any president since Hoover. In his first year (1969) he held eight, and in 1970 he held only six. If he thought no one was counting he was wrong. Both newsmen and political observers expressed shock and outrage as this practice (or non-practice) continued throughout his administration.[104] Herb Klein, Nixon's Director of Communications, maintained that there was so much the President had to know before he faced a press conference, the President needed a lot of time to prepare. That is the reason why Nixon held so few.[105] However, as one notes from F. D. R.'s twice weekly sessions, a large volume of concerns and issues is often reason to hold more press conferences, not less.

With the conflicting reports on American activities in Vietnam and Cambodia and then the self-bugging and Watergate disclosures, there was mounting pressure within the press to get information and on Nixon to give it. Nixon finally held an open-air session at Sam Clemente in August of 1973 after not having had a conference for over five months. The questions were so hostile and unreleting that Nixon walked off the stage before the usual "Thank you, Mr. President."[106]

It was in Nixon's conferences that reporter's questions became openly adversarial. Nixon stooped to sparring publicly with Dan Rather, each attempting to belittle the other. For the first time in the history of the sessions one finds disrespect on the part of both President and the press. Nixon's October 26, 1973 meeting represents the lowest level of exchange. Rather asked if the President should not be impeached, given recent events. Nixon said, "Well, I am glad we don't take a vote in this room." During the same session Robert Pierpoint asked Nixon why reporters seemed to upset him so much, to which Nixon replied it was not true. Pierpoint pressed the matter and Nixon responded, "You can't get angry at someone you don't respect."

Eisenhower had asked how a reporter could ever hurt a President and Nixon's experience shows how it can be done. Both Johnson and Nixon had collapsed the distance between the President and reporters. Distrust and disrespect reduced the President to a man "hiding behind his words."[107] For the first time one hears in various descriptions of the President's press conference that it exposed "Presidential vulnerability."[108] If the press conference could be the pulpit for a Teddy Roosevelt, it could also be a snare for those who have much to hide.

President Ford held his first press conference nineteen days after taking office. Prior to this meeting he had held several days of long press briefings.[109] In Ford's autobiography he says he had totally misguessed what the reporters would ask him; he believed that Nixon would not be an issue because "his fate was up to the Special Prosecutor and the courts."[110] To Ford's great alarm, all the reporters asked him about was Nixon. It was this startling encounter which Ford claims led him to grant the pardon; Ford wanted the country to get on with other affairs and not to be paralyzed for months and months over a criminal trial of Nixon.[111]

However, even after the pardon the presidential press conference remained a virtual cross-examination. Not only did reporters want to challenge repeatedly Ford's justification for the pardon, they also wanted to know such things as who paid the President's golfing fees, the President or the public?[112] They would ask why was Ford not his usual cheerful self, when it happened to be two months before the election and Ford's income tax records were suspect.[113] Correspondents appeared to vie for the honor of asking the most telling question, the worth of which was measured by the degree of discomfiture it caused. These sessions had become a proving ground for investigative journalists.

Yet despite the fallout of Watergate, Ford's press conference record is one of initiative and innovation. He wished to get away from the cold formality. Press Secretary ter Horst made some suggestions to that end. Ford has related them:

> One was to move reporters' chairs closer to the podium so as to reduce the sense of 'distance' between the President and the press. Another was to discard the blue curtain that Nixon had always stood in front of -- it looked stagy and imperial -- and to position me on the other side of the East Room before open doors that led to the red-carpeted Grand Entrance Hall. That, predicted ter Horst, would create a much friendlier atmosphere.[114]

Ford also differentiated himself from Nixon by holding more frequent sessions. In his two and a half years in office he held forty-one conferences; they occurred at least once and often twice a month. Almost half were outside of Washington.

Ford varied the site of the press conferences. Of the twenty-one he had on White House grounds, five were in the East Room, five in Room 450 of the Old Executive Office Building, three in the Rose Garden, two in the Briefing Room, two on the South Grounds, two in the Oval Office, and one on the North Lawn. Ford also met with the press at varying times -- in the mornings, afternoons, or evenings.

Ford has claimed to be the first President to hold a press conference just for the local press; this meeting occurred in Atlanta on November 14, 1975. The evidence suggests that his assertion is correct. Many of his press conferences outside of Washington had either no live radio or T.V. coverage or were only broadcast live on regional television and radio networks.

One of the most prominent innovations during the Ford administration was the regular practice of reporters asking follow-up questions. The beginning of 1975 on is when one first notes a marked increase in follow-ups. A reporter usually asks a question and adds that he has one or two to follow. Another way of going about the same thing is for the correspondent to remain standing and in this way he indicates he is not finished.[105]

Ford's press conferences broke one other tradition. As already noted, television networks want to avoid running overtime and this places certain constraints on these sessions. Ford, however, discarded this artificial timeline once by remaining after the "Thank you, Mr. President" and answering questions after the cameras were turned off.[116]

The changes which took place within Ford's conferences are descriptive of both a president and a press corps made more wary in the aftermath of Watergate. For correspondents that meant pinning the President down; for Ford that meant being more open and outgoing. Both wished to fortify their positions in light of what the previous administration had wrought.

President Jimmy Carter stated at his first press conference that he would hold meetings with the press twice a month. He described press conferences at his first sessions as "confrontations ... to kind of balance the nice and pleasant things that come to me as President."[117] The bywords were no longer "presidential leadership," but instead Carter spoke of "open government" and "honesty in office." His conferences in effect were to perform the function of informal trials before a jury. In May of 1977 Carter said:

> [There] has been a loss of confidence in our Government, both in its integrity and also in its ability and competence ... So a major commitment of mine ... was to try to restore the confidence of the people in me. Obviously, one of these means is by frequent news conferences ... And the openness with which I hope I am conducting my administration means that we don't try to cover up our mistakes.[118]

From this statement one sees that Carter's public understanding of the press conference's purpose was a far cry from that of the Roosevelts and Kennedy. The conference for Carter was an open forum, not a private seminar, in which the President must inevitably be on the defensive.

Carter usually held his press conferences in Room 450 of the Old Executive Office Building. During his first year in office he preferred 10:00 AM and 2:30 PM sessions; in 1978 and 1979 he moved to 4:00 PM; and in 1980 his news conferences usually met at 8:00 or 9:00 PM. All of the ones which he held in Washington received live national television converage, as did many of those he held outside of the nation's capitol.

Several hundred reporters attended Carter's press conferences. One veteran correspondent described the meetings as being too large but asks, "How are you going to make them smaller?"[119] Indeed, the Wilsonian legacy of open access tenaciously held. As a result of the magnitude of the event the presidential press conference evolved to become much more formal than it was even under so recent a President as Kennedy. These meetings grew so much more stylized than those of F. D. R. to make the two formats incomparable.

Seats for correspondents were assigned. The seniors and regulars sat in the front rows, the others toward the back.[120] Carter knew the old hands and could anticipate their questions.[121] Those in the back were usually left out. Ray Scherer believes that this is the reason why the foreign press no longer participated -- as a rule they sat further back and thus could not compete for recognition.[122]

Though the presidential press conference received more attention and importance than ever before, one finds that on the whole it had become a more shallow event. Many reporters attended these sessions but more and more stayed home and just watched on T.V. Scherer says people stayed away because the conferences were "not as rewarding as they used to be in bringing out the President's personality."[123] The increased formality had created greater distance and less information. Even the follow-up question, frequent at first but later discouraged by Carter,[124] did not result in more spontaneous dialogue. Reporters always asked pre-selected questions, whether they were follow-ups or not, and all genuine continuity was lost.[125]

Yet it is impossible to believe that the presidential press conference had been reduced to a mere formality. As Michael Grossman and Margaret Kumar state in a recent article, the presidential press conference is still a "high-risk forum." At the time Grossman and Kumar wrote, Carter still held his sessions on a monthly basis. They predicted such regularity would not last.[126] The margin for embarassment and negative press increases over time to the point where a President judges it to be more beneficial to cut back on these sessions.

Carter later bore out this prediction. Up until July 1978 he continued to meet with reporters as often as he had initially promised. Thereafter he held his news conferences once a month until July 25, 1979. In this conference Carter announced that he wanted more contact with non-Washington reporters. He hoped thereby to escape the narrow focus of the Washington professionals:

> I would like to let my voice be heard and felt and the questions be heard by me and felt from various placed in the country.[127]

He held only two official press conferences (as opposed to town meetings and other sessions with reporters) for the remainder of that year, one in mid-October and the other on November 28, 1979, and he had only six in 1980. All were in Washington.

When President Ronald Reagan took office in 1981, he was open to suggestions on how he could improve the presidential press conference. Within the first month of his administration, the White Burkett Miller Center of Public Affairs at the University of Virginia made available to the President a report on the subject. During the previous year, the Center had organized and sponsored a Commission on Presidential Press Conferences. The Commission's report recommended that

1) The president should hold televised press conferences, with open access, once a month.

2) The president should have weekly informal sessions, using whatever format he deems appropriate (i.e., without television or radio equipment, if he chooses).

3) At the regular sessions, have the reporters raise their hands rather than leap and shout.

4) Questioners at the monthly press conferences could be chosen by lot.[128]

The intent of these recommendations was to allow the presidential press conference to yield better information on a consistent basis in a manner which benefits both the president and the press.

The evidence suggests that Reagan was in accord with this intent and thought that these recommendations would be effective. To quote a recent Washington Post article, the study's recommendations "have been acted upon with a speed not usually seen in connection with reports of private groups submitted to the White House."[129] On January 29, 1981, the date of President Reagan's first press conference, reporters raised their hands to be recognized.

Mr. James Brady, Reagan's press secretary, has said that the President's second session will use the lottery system -- only randomly preselected reporters will ask questions.[130] There are also reports that Mr. Reagan intends to hold informal press conferences as well.[131] It will be interesting indeed to see if these changes will yield the benefits they are intended to produce. Whatever the results, the presidential press conference continues to evolve.

THE ROLES AND FUNCTIONS OF THE PRESIDENTIAL PRESS CONFERENCE

Thus, there appear to be interesting tensions within the presidential press conference as it exists today. The sessions are a result of presidential initiative -- a President says how, when, and where, and he may choose not to answer any question. President Reagan's reforms clearly illustrate that the President decides how these meetings will be conducted. On the other hand, one finds that since Kennedy, presidents do not seem to enjoy these meetings. Grossman and Kumar have described the cycle of initial enthusiasm for and gradual disenchantment with the press conference in each presidency.[132] The conferences have tended to become "confrontations" which a President cannot avoid but which he inevitably makes less frequent. The question is, if the conferences are so clearly within the control of the President, why do they remain the "high risk forum" Grossman and Kumar describe them to be? The answer may be that as presidents since F. D. R. have, in these sessions, taken greater and greater strides to speak directly to the people, they have increasingly lost the control earlier presidents exercised over the news generated in their press conferences.

Moreover, the press conference as an institution has so far proven itself to be more expansive than elastic. It does not easily spring back once it has been stretched. Kennedy's decision to broadcast his press conferences live gave him the means to reach the public in the most effective way hitherto possible with modern technology. His ability matched his ambition. President Johnson, however, did not feel comfortable with live television broadcasts, yet he was ultimately unsuccessful at instituting other formats. He could not meet the demands initiated by his predecessor and the slack reflected badly on him. Indeed, it is interesting to contrast L. B. J. with Reagan. Like Johnson, Reagan intends to have non-televised press conferences as already stated. Unlike L. B. J., however, Reagan is at his ease before cameras. Johnson floundered for some way to escape stagefright, and failed. Reagan approaches his experiments with press conferences from a position of strength -- he already comes across well on television. Perhaps the changes he institutes will therefore fare better and be longer lived than those of Johnson.

As it stands today the public expects to see and hear presidential press conferences as they occur. Since Kennedy, no president has ventured to challenge completely or change totally that expectation. Since Teddy Roosevelt started the whole business only Taft flatly refused to hold any at all, and he had the advantage of not having to battle the weight of tradition. From observations of recent Presidents it would appear that if the man in office found aggressive leadership within his press conferences too risky or unbecoming, the tendency has been to be on the defensive. Rather than meet the press on his own terms, the purpose has been to show the people he can take anything reporters can dish out.

In looking at the growth and evolution of these sessions it is clear that television has wrought the most far-reaching changes. Yet television did not radically transform the press conference, it simply exaggerated tendencies which were already present. Before F. D. R., the press conferences had been sometimes more and sometimes less formal, sometimes using written questions or allowing direct quotation and sometimes not. F. D. R. increased censor and decreased formality. Under Truman the formality increased somewhat and censor decreased -- he allowed delayed radio broadcasts of the sessions. Eisenhower continued the drift of the previous administration. The U. S. had blossomed into a full world power and as a result the press conference was a matter of great import. The times demanded wider exposure of the meetings and increased the consequences of misspeaking. Pre-press conference briefings, begun under Truman, grew more intense; the setting was more formalized; and the President permitted delayed television broadcast.

Thus, Kennedy's televised conferences were another step in an established progression. With his administration, the emphasis shifted gradually from news to personalities. If at first the televised meetings worked largely to the President's advantage, Johnson and Nixon inadvertently shifted the balance of control within their conferences to where it appeared they were not the captains but rather the captives. Individual correspondents found they could use the press conference as a means to personal fame. Recent presidents have tried to cultivate an image through their handling of reporters. A recent New York Times editorial noted this practice and described how Carter pursued it:

> Some Presidents have consciously played on the scene of leaping, shouting reporters, as if to say to the public, look at how unruffled and authoritative I am even before this herd of barking animals. Jimmy Carter seemed to relish the contrast: recall his skillful handling of hostile Billy Carter questions at an hour-long news conference last August.[133]

As it has stood until recently, the press conference has been as much a stage as it has been a forum. The effects and durability of Mr. Reagan's reforms have yet to be determined.

How does one evaluate this evolution? What function does the presidential press conference play in the American political system? Some political observers -- Max Way and Joseph Loftus for example -- believe that the practice has no significant place in the political scheme at all. Those of this persuasion say there are myriad ways a President can communicate with the public; thus, the regularity or even absence of press conferences does not make much of a difference. The press can get the President to respond through other means. The way newspapers dealt with Taft was to attack him in editorials and place the burden of clarification or rebuttal on his shoulders.[134]

Moreover, say those in this camp, the press does not represent the only pressure upon the President to speak. For example, a Congressional speech or an interview with a disgruntled staff member can also place pressure on the President to respond. This view does not see the press conference as filling any unique niche in the American government system. If the President wants to drop his conferences he should be able to do so without explanation or loss.[135]

Yet why does this type of thinking raise the hackles of most reporters, political observers, and even of some Presidents? The general feeling now is not much different than what Merriman Smith set forth in 1946:

> But should there come some day to the White House a President who thinks he can drop press conferences -- well, he's President and he can do pretty much what he wants. But what a skull beating he's in for! His honeymoon will last exactly up to the time he says, 'No press conference' ...[136]

What is it about the presidential press conference that makes it so valuable to so many?

One way of understanding the press conference is to say it is or should be a conduit for accurate information between the President and the public, represented by the press. Though there are other ways of communicating facts, these sessions are unique in that the President may explain in length or personally clarify an issue or event. The President is there as the horse's mouth, so to speak. According to this view, the reporters' role is to ask the most pertinent questions. They are not there to trip up the President. In turn, the President is obliged to give direct and clear answers to the extent that it is possible. He is not to conduct his conferences while roaming around the White House or while having a barbeque. He should use those formats which open themselves up the least to possible distortion.

Moreover, the press conference is not just a matter of the President's bringing the facts to bear on a situation. It is also an occasion for him to learn. Ford learned how preoccupied the nation was with Nixon when he stepped into that first press conference. In Truman's last meeting with the press he said his conferences allowed him to know what was uppermost in the minds of other political observers -- reporters. George Reedy, commenting on Johnson's press conferences, said the sessions were most valuable in preventing the President from becoming isolated. The correspondents, he believes, keep the President's perspective in touch with reality.[137]

Accurate information, this view stresses, is crucial because of the audience. The perils of misspeaking are greatest in matters of foreign policy. Presidents respond to this situation in different ways. Nixon said he would not discuss foreign policy "off-the-cuff" in press conferences. Kennedy, however, openly stated his positions precisely because he knew America's enemies were listening.

People who believe in the press conference as an exchange between the White House and the press for the sake of knowledge feel ill-served by present usage. Reporters and presidents often care only to be self-serving. The rise of investigative and specialized reporting leads toward biased questions, distorted information, or not covering the truly important matters. Correspondents have all their questions worked out beforehand. Presidents now also come into their press conferences knowing exactly what they will say. The results are unsatisfactory on both sides. Presidents often do not answer the most provocative aspects of a question. Reporters often allow the President to get away with superficiality because their questions, even the follow-up ones, are predetermined. Both parties are unwilling to go with the drift of thought.

There are others who disagree with the "accurate information" school. Many think the press conference best serves the American people when it embodies a power struggle between the President and the press. The sessions thus become an extra-Constitutional form of checks and balances. The groups who think of the press conference in this way split, however, on who should mostly dominate, the press or the President.

Not surprisingly, those who favor the President were more prevalent prior to Johnson and Nixon. Advocates for an energetic presidency saw the need for concentration of power in the Oval Office; the events of the 1930's and 40's called for a President who would lead the world. Kennedy was probably the last president to enjoy virtually unlimited prerogatives.

Elmer Cornwell is perhaps the foremost proponent of this view. He believed that the presidential press conference should be one of many tools which the President uses to lead public opinion. According to Cornwell, this practice is not only a good thing but also vitally important. Presidents should avail themselves of every possible means to persuade the public to their point of view; they must wring every legitimate advantage they can out of the "bully pulpit" of the White House. If they do not,

> governmental vigor will certainly flag, and they will be abdicating their responsibility to their office, to the nation, and perhaps to the free world.[138]

If the President does not try to take advantage of his press conferences, then he courts more danger than if he were to do so without great effect.

Thus, the evolution of direct access to the viewing public through media coverage was a desirable development if one holds to Cornwell's view. The presidential press conference should be a bully pulpit; it should be a propaganda tool to draw popular support, especially if the President is opposed by Congress or the press. The President's goal is to use his conferences to bring public pressure to bear on others in behalf of the President. Presidents since Truman have often used their prepared opening statements to this purpose.

From this particular perspective, the press conference is the President's and he may work with it as he sees fit. It is a powerful channel of influence and therefore should not be discarded. The President should use his own discretion on the appropriate format and should answer questions in a self-serving way. The press play the role of bringing out the views of the President.

Those of the opposing view, the ones who favor the press in the power struggle, see the presidential press conference as a means by which the public can hold the President accountable. This belief has always existed side by side with the other view but only recently has it become the prevalent popular opinion. Merriman Smith was a journalist who covered the most energetic president of this century. Yet Smith believed the press conference was a check even on F. D. R. Smith wrote,

> Our Chief Executives do not always like the idea, but the American citizen has a direct property right in the Presidency. And it is the reporter assigned to the White House who keeps the people

up to date on what and how their property is doing.[139]

According to this perspective, reporters are in the press conference as representatives of the people. They are there to make sure the President acts responsively and responsibly.

Over time the press has evolved to become a force to deal with in their own right. In one of J. F. K.'s press conferences he once referred to the press as "the fourth estate."[140] And the body of correspondents can and often do serve an adversarial role. They are now informed critics of the government and better able to ask the harder questions than might be the ordinary citizen. The press conference is thus the American version of the British Prime Minister's stand before Parliament.

As stated earlier, this view of the President's press conferences is not incompatible with the position favoring presidential dominance. The press conference can be an arena within which a President tests his strength against a worthy foe. The encounter with the press need not diminish his leadership one bit. F. D. R. enjoyed the contest, and seemed, in Mr. Rowe's opinion,

> a little bit like a bull fighter with bulls. They were after him and he just enjoyed it. He kept pushing them right off into the corner. The pleasure he took out of coping with them I think was important.[141]

At Truman's last press conference he responded to the question of whether the sessions should be changed in any way. Truman answered no and went on to say, "I like this rough and tumble press conference we have right here. If I can't take care of myself, that's my fault."[142]

One of the main concerns of the people who believe in open government, however, is that the press conference gets the kind of information which, left to his own devices, the President would not give. Woodrow Wilson, though not particularly fond of reporters, believed they were a necessary burden. Thus, Wilson allowed equal access and open questioning. How else was the President to be held fully accountable on a continual basis?

It was not until the Johnson/Nixon years that this watchdog function evolved into open antagonism. Watergate was evidence that the presidency had acquired too much power. Some reporters looked back and saw Kennedy's press conferences as the root of all evil. The impact of the live coverage marked the beginning of the Imperial Presidency, some said; it was the touch which shifted the constitutional balance heavily in favor of the President.[143]

Moreover, reporters found investigative reporting could take one a long ways. Woodward and Bernstein are now celebrities, among the wealthiest members of their profession. Today the presidential press conference is virtually dominated by questions which probe personal as well as public aspects of the President's life. Reporters drill Carter on such things as who pays for and has access to the White House tennis courts as if the answers to these questions could unearth another Watergate.[144]

Another understanding of the press conference's role is that it is a means of assessing the President's personal character. Throughout this paper's historical survey, one has seen how the presidential press conference is in part a reflection of the President's personality. In these meetings reporters, and now the general public, get a sense of the man by seeing him in action. The setting of the press conference is the crucial feature, for here the President confronts knowledgeable critics. He must spontaneously field their questions. From these impromptu interactions, the people judge how well the President thinks on his feet and maintains his poise.

It is the image the President projects in live press conferences that is perhaps what strikes everyone. Yet in truth this effect of the press conference is the most spurious. These sorts of exchanges can never present a comprehensive reflection of the man. Some, like Johnson, may just not do well before cameras or reporters; the setting may inhibit some presidents and allow others to flourish. The quick repartee and the glib response are not measures of how well a President rules. The presidential press conference shows how a man appears under a certain set of conditions. It would be wrong to extrapolate from these sessions an entire personality profile of the man. As Douglas Carter stated recently, "Being a quick study is only one aspect of potential leadership."[145]

However, presidential advisers know that no one can watch a live broadcast of a press conference without making character judgments. With this in mind, the effort is to capitalize on the occasion by projecting a "favorable" image regardless of whether it happens to be a true one or not. Ever since Kennedy's success as a "personality," the White House has placed increased importance on the dramatic aspect of the press conferences, engaging the services of professional acting coaches and the like. As a result, the press conference is more of a show, a concerted effort to create a deliberate effect.

Hence, the press conference performs many different functions, each overlapping the other. The sessions are always a source of news, though different presidents have used it more and some less as an information channel. At the same time all presidents have to some degree tried to use it as a means to influence the press, their own bureaucracy, Congress, the Courts, and ultimately the people in how they view presidential policy. Yet the same exposure which allows for leadership also permits the public to be witness to a cross-examination of the President. While all these various forces are at work within the press conference, the audience watches and makes some overall judgment of the President as a man. These different yet complimentary facets of the presidential press conference make it a unique institution within the system of American government.

All these roles, however, may be encompassed within a broader understanding of the press conference. As an unanticipated outgrowth of the American brand of democracy it is a valuable servant. Truman best summed up what the presidential press conference symbolizes and what purposes it serves. At the close of his last meeting with reporters he said,

> This kind of news conference where reporters can ask any question they can dream up -- directly of the President of the United States -- illustrates how strong and vital our democracy is. There is no other country in the world where the chief of state submits to such unlimited questioning. I know, too, from experience that it is not easy to stand up here and try to answer 'off the cuff' all kinds of questions without any advance notice. Perhaps succeeding Presidents will be able to figure out improvements and safeguards in the procedure. I hope they will never cut the direct line of communication between themselves and the people.[146]

So far Truman's final wish has not been disappointed.

Depending on personality, custom, and historical accident, different aspects of the press conferences have come to the fore. Yet all of its various roles exist in latent form regardless of which wanes and waxes at any given time. At least that is how it has appeared thus far. In the president's conferences one sees the struggle between the forces of open government and the forces of an energetic presidency. Ideally the two fight for dominance and thus bring both influences to bear upon the sessions. Consequently they provide the system with the benefits of each.

It is true that the presidential press conference is not unique as a channel of information nor is it the only vehicle for presidential leadership, accountability, or image-building. Yet when all these functions are combined within one institution it is clear why the presidential press conference has endured. In its present form it is in neither the President's interest to cease in holding them nor in the reporter's interest to stop attending. Precisely because the presidential press conference serves no one participant exclusively it serves the American people best.

NOTES

[1] Herbert Hoover, *Public Papers of the President* (Washington, D. C.: National Archives and Records Services), press conference of March 5, 1929.

[2] Elmer E. Cornwell, Jr., *Presidential Leadership of Public Opinion* (Bloomington, Indiana: Indiana University Press, 1966), P. 17.

[3] Ibid., p. 19.

[4] Ibid., p. 18.

[5] Ibid., pp. 19-20.

[6] M. L. Stein, *When Presidents Meet The Press* (New York: Julian Messmer, 1969), p. 45.

[7] Cornwell, p. 28.

[8] Stein, pp. 51-52.

[9] Cornwell, pp. 36-37. Wilson met with reporters once or twice weekly until mid-July of 1915, when he ceased to hold press conferences at all for well over a year, and then irregularly thereafter.

[10] Ibid., p. 37.

[11] Ibid., p. 36.

[12] Ibid., p. 45.

[13] Ibid., pp. 55-59.

[14] Ibid., p. 64.

[15] Ibid.

[16] Fred Essary, quoted in Cornwell, p. 64.

[17] Ibid., p. 65.

[18] Ibid., p. 67.

[19] Cornwell, pp. 75-78.

[20] Ibid., p. 80.

[21] Ibid., pp. 87-88; Transcript of March 20, 1980, p. 4 and p. 10.

[22] Cornwell, pp. 78-88; Transcript of March 20, 1980, p. 10.

[23] Hoover, press conference of March 5, 1929.

[24] William W. Lammers, "Presidential Press Conference Schedules: Who Hides, and When?" (paper presented at the 1979 Annual Meeting of the American Political Science Association, August 31 - September 1, 1979), p. 6.

[25] Cornwell, p. 106.

[26] Ibid., p. 108.

[27] Basil Rauch, editor, <u>Franklin D. Roosevelt: Selected Speeches, Messages, Press Conferences, and Letters</u>, (New York: Holt, Reinhard and Winston, 1964), p. 95.

[28] Pierre Salinger, <u>With Kennedy</u>, (Garden City, N.J.: Doubleday and Co., 1966), p. 139.

[29] Cornwell, p. 143.

[30] Ibid., pp. 157-160.

[31] Transcript of a press conference forum held on March 20, 1980, by the White Burkett Miller Center of Public Affairs at the University of Virginia, p. 13.

[32] Cornwell, pp. 157-158; Transcript of March 30, 1980, p. 51.

[33] Transcript of March 30, 1980, p. 12.

[34] Ibid., p. 15.

[35] Cornwell, p. 150.

[36] Transcript of March 20, 1980, p. 16.

[37] Cornwell, p. 161.

[38] Salinger, p. 139.

[39]Ray Scherer, "The Presidential Press Conference," The Virginia Papers on the Presidency: The White Burkett Miller Center Forum, 1979, Editor Kenneth Thompson (Washington, D. C.: University Press of America, Inc., 1979), p. 68; Transcript of March 30, 1980, p. 78.

[40]Salinger, p. 59.

[41]Harry Truman, The Public Papers of the President (Washington, D. C.: National Archives and Records Service), press conference of January 15, 1953.

[42]Scherer, p. 69.

[43]Salinger, pp. 55-56.

[44]Scherer, p. 67.

[45]Stephen Hess, Organizing the Presidency (Washington, D. C.: The Brookings Institution, 1976), p. 51; Transcript of March 30, 1980, p. 32.

[46] The Presidency and the Press Conference, Rational Debate Seminars (Washington, D. C.: American Enterprise Institute for Public Policy Research, 1971), p. 10.

[47]Ibid., p. 10.

[48]Merriman Smith, Thank You, Mr. President: A White House Notebook (New York: Harper and Brothers Publishers, 1946), p. 29; James E. Pollard, "The News Conference As A Communication Challenge," The Public Opinion Quarterly (Winter 1951-1952), p. 668.

[49]Scherer, pp. 67-68.

[50]Cornwell, p. 178 and p. 187.

[51] The Presidency and the Press, Editor Hayt Purvis (Austin, Texas: The University of Texas at Austin, 1976), p. 10.

[52]Scherer, p. 68.

[53]Ibid., p. 69.

[54]Transcript of March 20, 1980, p. 15.

[55] Salinger, pp. 55-56.

[56] Ibid., p. 59.

[57] Hess, p. 64.

[58] Transcript of March 20, 1980, p. 90.

[59] The Presidency and the Press Conference, pp. 19-20.

[60] Dwight D. Eisenhower, Public Papers of the President (Washington, D. C.: National Archives and Records Service), see press conferences of September 30 and December 16, 1953.

[61] The Presidency and the Press, p. 12.

[62] Ibid.

[63] Eisenhower's press conference of January 18, 1960.

[64] Transcript of March 20, 1980, p. 139.

[65] Salinger, p. 56.

[66] Ibid.

[67] Transcript of March 20, 1980, p. 15.

[68] Salinger, pp. 57-58.

[69] Ibid., p. 59.

[70] Ibid., p. 57.

[71] Ibid., pp. 57-58.

[72] John F. Kennedy, Public Papers of the President (Washington, D. C.: National Archives and Record Service), press conference of March 8, 1961.

[73] Kennedy's press conference of March 1, 1961.

[74] Salinger, p. 140.

[75] Ibid., pp. 137-138.

[76] The Presidency and the Press, p. 11.

[77] Transcript of March 20, 1980, pp. 136-137.

[78] The Presidency and the Press Conference, pp. 16-17.

[79] Salinger, p. 112.

[80] Ibid.

[81] Ibid., pp. 337-338.

[82] Scherer, p. 70.

[83] Transcript of March 20, 1980.

[84] The Presidency and the Press, pp. 13-14.

[85] Lyndon B. Johnson, Public Papers of the President (Washington, D. C.: National Archives and Record Service), press conference of March 20, 1965.

[86] The Johnson Presidential Press Conferences, Editor Doris Kearns, Vol. I (New York: Earl M. Coleman Enterprises, Inc., 1978), p. i.

[87] Ibid., p. iii.

[88] Ibid., p. ii.

[89] Ibid., p. vii.

[90] Salinger, p. 339.

[91] The Presidency and the Press Conference, p. 48.

[92] Transcript of March 20, 1980, p. 49.

[93] The Johnson Presidential Press Conferences, p. iv.

[94] Ibid.

[95] Ibid., p. vi.

[96] Ibid.

[97] Ibid., p. vii.

[98]Michael Grossman and Martha Kumar, "Milton's Army: The White House Press Corps" (paper delivered at the 1979 Annual Meeting of the American Political Science Association, August 31 - September 3, 1979), p. 8.

[99]George Reedy, The Twilight of the Presidency, (New York: The World Publishing Co., 1970), p. 164.

[100]The Presidency and the Press Conferences, p. 49.

[101]Gerald R. Ford, A Time to Heal, (New York: Harper and Row, 1979), pp. 156-157.

[102]The Nixon Presidential Press Conferences, Editor Helen Thomas (New York: Earl M. Coleman Enterprises, Inc., 1978), p. ii.

[103]Nixon's press conference of January 27, 1969.

[104] The Presidency and the Press Conference, p. 12.

[105]Ibid., p. 37.

[106]The Nixon Presidential Press Conferences, pp. i-ii.

[107]Scherer, p. 85.

[108] The Nixon Presidential Press Conferences, Editor's Introduction.

[109]Ford, A Time to Heal, p. 157.

[110]Ibid.

[111]Ibid.

[112]Gerald R. Ford, Public Papers of the President, (Washington, D. C.: National Archives and Record Service), press conference of September 30, 1976.

[113]Ibid., press conference of October 14, 1976.

[114]Ford, A Time to Heal, pp. 156-157.

[115]The Nixon Presidential Press Conferences, p. iv.

[116]Ford's press conference of December 20, 1975.

[117]Jimmy Carter, Public Papers of the President, (Washington, D. C.: National Archives and Record Service), press conference of February 8, 1977.

[118] Ibid., press conference of May 12, 1977.

[119] Scherer, p. 74.

[120] Ibid., p. 89.

[121] Ibid., p. 73.

[122] Ibid., p. 89.

[123] Ibid., p. 74.

[124] Transcript April 24, 1980, p. 13.

[125] Scherer, p. 74.

[126] Michael Grossman and Martha Kumar, "The Media and the Presidency: An Exchange Analysis," Political Science Quarterly (Spring 1979), p. 45.

[127] Carter's press conference of July 25, 1979.

[128] Report of the Commission on the Presidential Press Conferences, (Washington, D. C.: University Press of America, Inc., 1981), pp. 4-6.

[129] The Washington Post, January 31, 1981, p. 2.

[130] Ibid.

[131] The New York Times, February 8, 1981, p. E18.

[132] Grossman and Kumar, "The Media and the Presidency: An Exchange Analysis."

[133] The New York Times, February 8, 1981, p. E18.

[134] Stein, p. 52.

[135] See Max Way's discussion in The Presidency and the Press Conference, pp. 12, 35, and 55; also, Joseph Loftus, pp. 40-41.

[136] Smith, p. 29.

[137] Reedy, p. 165.

[138] Cornwell, pp. 7-8.

[139]Smith, p. i.

[140]Kennedy's press conference of May 9, 1962.

[141]Transcript of March 20, 1980, p. 40.

[142]Truman's press conference of January 15, 1953.

[143] <u>The Kennedy Presidential Press Conferences</u>, Editor David Halberstam (New York: Earl M. Coleman Enterprises, Inc., 1978), p. iii.

[144]Carter's press conference of April 30, 1979.

[145]Transcript of April 24, 1980, p. 102.

[146]Truman's press conference of January 15, 1953.

BIBLIOGRAPHY

Carter, Jimmy. Public Papers of the President. Washington, D. C.: National Archives and Record Service.

Cornwell, Elmer E., Jr. Presidential Leadership of Public Opinion. Bloomington, Indiana: Indiana University Press, 1966.

Eisenhower, Dwight D. Public Papers of the President. Washington, D. C.: National Archives and Records Service.

Ford, Gerald R. A Time to Heal. New York: Harper and Row, 1979.

_____. Public Papers of the President. Washington, D. C.: National Archives and Record Service.

Grossman, Michael and Martha Kumar. "Milton's Army: The White House Press Corps." Paper prepared for delivery at the 1979 Annual Meeting of the American Political Science Association, August 31 - September 3, 1979.

_____. "The Media and the Presidency: An Exchange Analysis." Political Science Quarterly. Spring 1979.

Hess, Stephen. Organizing the Presidency. Washington, D. C.: The Brookings Institution, 1976.

Hoover, Herbert. Public Papers of the President. Washington, D. C.: National Archives and Records Service.

Johnson, Lyndon. Public Papers of the President. Washington, D. C.: National Archives and Records Service.

_____. The Johnson Presidential Press Conferences. Editor Doris Kearns. Volume 1 and 2. New York: Earl M. Coleman Enterprises, Inc., 1978.

Kennedy, John F. Public Papers of the President. Washington, D. C.: National Archives and Records Service.

_____. The Kennedy Presidential Press Conferences. Editor David Halberstam. New York: Earl M. Coleman Enterprises, Inc., 1978.

Lammers, William W. "Presidential Press Conference Schedules: Who Hides, and When?" Paper prepared for delivery at the 1979 Annual Meeting of the American Political Science Association, August 31 - September 3, 1979.

Nixon, Richard M. Public Papers of the President. Washington, D. C.: National Archives and Records Service.

_____. The Nixon Presidential Press Conferences. Editor David Halberstam. New York: Earl M. Coleman Enterprises, Inc., 1978.

Pollard, James E. "The News Conference As A Communication Channel." The Public Opinion Quarterly. Winter 1951-52, pp. 663-678.

The Presidency and the Press Conference. Rational Debate Seminars. Washington, D. C.: American Enterprise Institute for Public Policy Research, 1971.

Purvis, Hoyt. Editor. The Presidency and the Press. Austin, Texas: The University of Texas at Austin, 1976.

Reedy, George. The Twilight of the Presidency. New York: The World Publishing Co., 1970.

Report of the Commission on Presidential Press Conferences. Sponsored by the White Burkett Miller Center of Public Affairs at the University of Virginia. Washington, D. C.: University Press of America, Inc., 1981.

Roosevelt, Franklin D. Completed Presidential Press Conferences of Franklin D. Roosevelt. New York: De Capo Press, 1972.

_____. Roosevelt: Selected Speeches, Messages, Press Conferences, and Letters. New York: Holt, Rinehart and Winston, 1964.

Salinger, Pierre. With Kennedy. Garden City, N.Y.: Doubleday and Co., 1966.

Scherer, Ray. "The Presidential Press Conference." The Virginia Papers on the Presidency: The White Burkett Miller Center Forum, 1979. Editor Kenneth Thompson. Washington, D. C.: University Press of America, Inc., 1979, pp. 65-93.

Smith, Merriman. Thank you, Mr. President: A White House Notebook. New York: Harper and Brothers Publishers, 1946.

Stein, M. L. When Presidents Meet the Press. New York: Julian Messmer, 1969.

Transcripts of press conferences forums held on March 20, April 24, and July 21 of 1980 by the White Burkett Miller Center of Public Affairs at the University of Virginia.

Truman, Harry. <u>Public Papers of the President</u>. Washington, D. C.: National Archives and Records Service.

E 743 .F73